DECISIONS

SEEKING GOD'S GUIDANCE

DONALD BAKER

9 STUDIES
FOR INDIVIDUALS
OR GROUPS

T0386146

INTER-VARSITY PRESS
36 Causton Street, London SW1P 4ST, England
Email: ivp@ivpbooks.com
Website: www.ivpbooks.com

*Originally published in the United States of America in the LifeGuide® Bible Studies series
in 2001 by InterVarsity Press, Downers Grove, Illinois
First published in Great Britain by Scripture Union in 2001
Second UK edition published in 2016
This edition published in Great Britain by Inter-Varsity Press 2019*

British Library Cataloguing-in-Publication Data
A catalogue record for this book is available from the British Library.

ISBN: 978–1–78359–845–8

Printed in Great Britain by Ashford Colour Press Ltd, Gosport, Hampshire

*Inter-Varsity Press publishes Christian books that are true to the Bible and that communicate
the gospel, develop discipleship and strengthen the church for its mission in the world.*

*IVP originated within the Inter-Varsity Fellowship, now the Universities and Colleges Christian
Fellowship, a student movement connecting Christian Unions in universities and colleges
throughout Great Britain, and a member movement of the International Fellowship of
Evangelical Students. Website: www.uccf.org.uk. That historic association is maintained,
and all senior IVP staff and committee members subscribe to the UCCF Basis of Faith.*

Contents

Getting the Most
Out of *Decisions*

Where should I go to school? What career should I choose? Who should I marry? How should I invest my money? Help! God has given me free will, and while I appreciate his confidence in my ability to choose, there are times when I wish that he would make the decisions for me. One wrong decision could seriously mess up my life. Why doesn't God just tell me what to do?

While the Bible cannot give us the answer to every decision that we face, it does teach us how to make decisions. Prayer, study, the leading of the Holy Spirit, circumstances, seeking advice and common sense are all involved. Still, there is no formula that works for every decision. God shows us the way in his own time and by his mysterious methods.

I have found that the constants in making wise decisions are (1) setting your desire on God and (2) patience.

The studies in this book were written while I have been struggling with decisions concerning my future. These Bible passages have been important to me as I have been knocking on God's door. As of this writing, I am still waiting, praying and listening.

I pray that you will hear God speaking to you through these studies, and that you will experience his guidance in the decisions that you face.

Suggestions for Individual Study

1. As you begin each study, pray that God will speak to you through his Word.

2. Read the introduction to the study and respond to the personal reflection question or exercise. This is designed to help you focus on God and on the theme of the study.

3. Each study deals with a particular passage—so that you can delve into the author's meaning in that context. Read and reread the passage to be studied. If you are studying a book, it will be helpful to read through the entire book prior to the first study. The questions are written using the language of the New International Version, so you may wish to use that version of the Bible. The New Revised Standard Version is also recommended.

4. This is an inductive Bible study, designed to help you discover for yourself what Scripture is saying. The study includes three types of questions. *Observation* questions ask about the basic facts: who, what, when, where and how. *Interpretation* questions delve into the meaning of the passage. *Application* questions help you discover the implications of the text for growing in Christ. These three keys unlock the treasures of Scripture.

Write your answers to the questions in the spaces provided or in a personal journal. Writing can bring clarity and deeper understanding of yourself and of God's Word.

5. It might be good to have a Bible dictionary handy. Use it to look up any unfamiliar words, names or places.

6. Use the prayer suggestion to guide you in thanking God for what you have learned and to pray about the applications that have come to mind.

7. You may want to go on to the suggestion under "Now or Later," or you may want to use that idea for your next study.

Suggestions for Members of a Group Study

1. Come to the study prepared. Follow the suggestions for individual study mentioned above. You will find that careful preparation will greatly enrich your time spent in group discussion.

2. Be willing to participate in the discussion. The leader of your group will not be lecturing. Instead, he or she will be encouraging the members of the group to discuss what they have learned. The leader will be asking the questions that are found in this guide.

3. Stick to the topic being discussed. Your answers should be based on the verses which are the focus of the discussion and not on outside authorities such as commentaries or speakers. These studies focus on a particular passage of Scripture. Only rarely should you refer to other portions of the Bible. This allows for everyone to participate in in-depth study on equal ground.

4. Be sensitive to the other members of the group. Listen attentively when they describe what they have learned. You may be surprised by their insights! Each question assumes a variety of answers. Many questions do not have "right" answers, particularly questions that aim at meaning or application. Instead the questions push us to explore the passage more thoroughly.

When possible, link what you say to the comments of others. Also, be affirming whenever you can. This will encourage some of the more hesitant members of the group to participate.

5. Be careful not to dominate the discussion. We are sometimes so eager to express our thoughts that we leave too little opportunity for others to respond. By all means participate! But allow others to also.

6. Expect God to teach you through the passage being discussed and through the other members of the group. Pray that you will have an enjoyable and profitable time together, but also that as a result of the study you will find ways that you can take action individually and/or as a group.

7. Remember that anything said in the group is considered confidential and should not be discussed outside the group unless specific permission is given to do so.

8. If you are the group leader, you will find additional suggestions at the back of the guide.

1

Why Is
God Silent?

Isaiah 58

An enemy of Joan of Arc once mocked her by jeering, "She says she hears God's voice; why don't I hear his voice?" It is reported that Joan replied, "Don't you wish you did?"

GROUP DISCUSSION. If you could ask God one question and be assured of an answer, what would it be?

PERSONAL REFLECTION. Why have you begun a Bible study on making decisions? Begin by praying that God will lead you in the decision you are facing.

In the year 537 B.C., Cyrus, King of Persia, allowed a small number of his Jewish captives to return to Jerusalem for the purpose of rebuilding the temple. The foundation for the new temple was quickly laid, but then the political situation became uncertain, circumstances interrupted, and economic troubles became so severe that the operation was discontinued. Isaiah 58 is a message for these confused and off-track people. *Read Isaiah 58.*

1. What frustrations do the people feel with God?

2. When have you felt a similar frustration with him?

3. What have the people done to try to gain God's guidance?

4. In what similar ways do people attempt to discover God's will today?

5. Why does God declare the people rebellious (v. 1)?

6. If the people's fasting was sincere, how would it have been different?

7. What is the connection between receiving God's guidance and a concern for justice?

8. What promises does God make in verses 8-14?

9. What are the requirements for receiving these promises?

10. Why might God be withholding his light from us as a nation?

from you as an individual?

11. What have you learned from this passage that will help you to discover God's will?

Take time to confess your lack of sincerity and to ask for God's light to break forth.

Now or Later

The letter to the Ephesians explains why many people have become ignorant of and separated from God. *Read Ephesians 4:17—5:21.*

What are the results of doing things our own way?

What behaviors are to characterize our new life as Christians?

Which of the commands in these verses are the most difficult for you to keep?

How will keeping these commands help you to hear the voice of God?

2

Hard & Painful Decisions

"We are not necessarily doubting," said C. S. Lewis, "that God will do the best for us; we are wondering how painful the best will turn out to be."

GROUP DISCUSSION. Describe a time when God's best has been painful for you. How has this experience affected you?

PERSONAL REFLECTION. Do you ever fear God's will? When and why?

The apostle Paul made a momentous decision to return to Jerusalem. Even though many Christians urged Paul not to go and warned him that he would be arrested in Jerusalem, still Paul remained convinced that this was what he should do. As he traveled, he made several brief stops to visit friends, explain his decision and say farewell. *Read Acts 20:17—21:14.*

1. If you had been in Paul's position, would you have gone to Jerusalem? Why or why not?

2. For Paul, what were the issues involved in his decision to go to Jerusalem?

3. What do you find admirable about Paul's convictions?

4. How are your convictions similar to or different from Paul's?

5. What price have you had to pay for your convictions?

6. If God wanted Paul to go to Jerusalem, why did the Holy Spirit give so many warnings not to go?

7. How did Paul's meetings with various communities of disciples encourage and prepare him to enter Jerusalem?

8. How has God encouraged and prepared you for difficult times in your life?

9. Many Christians expect God's will to be the most pleasant and trouble-free alternative, but from Paul's experience, that is apparently not so. What would be a better criteria for interpreting God's will?

10. In your decision-making process, have you usually been more concerned about personal comfort or following God? How has this been shown?

11. Verse 14 says that in the end, the disciples "gave up and said, 'The Lord's will be done.'" Why is it so often difficult to give in to the Lord's will?

---

12. What are you having difficulty giving up to God's will?

Pray for each person in your group who is facing a difficult or painful decision.

Now or Later

A vivid description of someone facing a painful decision is found in the story of Jesus at Gethsemane. *Read Mark 14:32-42.*

Compare and contrast Jesus' decision to go to the cross with Paul's decision to go to Jerusalem.

What encouragement do Jesus' and Paul's examples give you for facing your own painful choices?

What do you learn from these stories about how to encourage a friend who is facing a painful decision?

3

God's
Unique Plan

Romans 12

Because each of us is different, God's plan for each of us is also different. If we are to know that plan, we must know ourselves—our gifts, talents, strengths and shortcomings.

GROUP DISCUSSION. What gifts and talents have you observed in each member of your group? Have each member of your group take a turn to listen while the other members tell him or her what gifts they have seen evidenced.

PERSONAL REFLECTION. What has God made unique about you?

In the first eleven chapters of the book of Romans, Paul tells about the facts of the gospel. Beginning with chapter 12, he speaks of the practical implications of the gospel for our behavior. His words have much to say about God's plan and direction for our lives. *Read Romans 12.*

1. After reading this chapter, how would you define a "living sacrifice"?

2. Verse 2 says that being "transformed by the renewing of your mind" will allow us to "test and approve what God's will is." What is a renewed mind?

How does it differ from a mind that has been conformed "to the pattern of this world"?

3. How do our minds become either conformed or renewed?

4. What disciplines are helping you to renew your mind?

5. What responsibility do you have to "test and approve what God's will is"?

How can you take this responsibility seriously?

6. What do verses 3-8 teach about God's plan for the Christian community?

7. What is meant by making a "sober judgment" of yourself (v. 3)?

8. How will failure to do this lead you off track in understanding God's will?

9. As you look at yourself with "sober judgment," what do you believe to be your function and gifts in the body?

10. How has an understanding of your gifts helped you to "test and approve what God's will is"?

11. How do verses 9-21 tell us that we should be treating other people?

12. Why would it be futile to seek God's will if we are not being renewed in our love for others?

13. Continue to make a sober judgment of yourself by evaluating whether you have been conformed or transformed according to each of the ethical instructions in verses 9-21.

Ask God to be continually renewing your mind, and confess to him where you have been conformed to the pattern of this world.

Now or Later

Make a list of the spiritual gifts that are mentioned in Romans 12:6-8; 1 Corinthians 12:7-11, 27-31; and Ephesians 4:11-13. Write out a definition for each of these gifts. Which of these gifts has God given you?

4

The Anatomy of a Wise Decision

Proverbs 3:1-26

Although knowledge will help us in making decisions, it is even more critical that we choose wisely. Wisdom combines good judgment, knowledge, experience and understanding, but it is different than any of these.

GROUP DISCUSSION. Ask each member of the group to write a definition of wisdom. After listening to each definition, discuss how you would now change your answers.

PERSONAL REFLECTION. Who do you consider to be wise? How has his or her wisdom been demonstrated?

The book of Proverbs offers practical advice through poetry; short, pithy sayings; and vivid comparisons. The main point of the book is that we should always seek the wisdom of God. *Read Proverbs 3:1-26.*

---

1. This passage describes many benefits of wisdom. Which of them are most attractive to you?

2. According to verses 1-12, what characterizes a wise decision?

3. Why is a commitment to "love and faithfulness" (v. 3) important to making a wise decision?

4. Some people would argue that it is unwise to trust anyone but yourself. How would you answer them after reading verses 5-8?

5. Why is it wise to "honor the Lord with your wealth" (v. 9) instead of spending it on yourself?

How have you done this?

6. How do people today "despise the Lord's discipline" (v. 11)?

7. What role has God's discipline played in making you wiser (vv. 11-12)?

8. What makes wisdom so valuable (vv. 13-18)?

9. How can you "embrace" wisdom (v. 18)?

10. According to verses 19-26, what can wisdom accomplish?

11. In what ways are you like and unlike the person described in verses 21-26?

12. What can you do to become more like the wise person pictured here?

13. What have these proverbs taught you about wisdom and how to find it?

Pray for godly wisdom in the decisions you face.

Read Jesus' parable about wisdom and foolishness in *Matthew 7:24-27.*

The wise and foolish man both faced the same decision—where and how to build a house—but they made very different choices. What factors do you think influenced their decision-making process?

Why are so many foundations built on sand?

What does this parable teach you about making wise choices and avoiding foolish ones?

5

Good Advice

It is said that "advice is cheap," which is probably due to the fact that there are more people selling it than buying it. The book of Proverbs, however, encourages us to value advice when it teaches, "Listen to advice and accept instruction, and in the end you will be wise" (19:20).

GROUP DISCUSSION. What is the best and worst advice you have been given? What happened when you followed each?

PERSONAL REFLECTION. How do you normally react to people who give you advice: (a) appreciative? (b) resentful? (c) indifferent? (d) skeptical? What does this tell you about yourself?

2 Timothy is a letter the apostle Paul wrote to a young pastor he had trained. In it, he encourages Timothy to stand strong in a world full of godlessness, false teaching and bad advice. *Read 2 Timothy 3:10—4:8.*

---

1. What information does Paul give about his character and suffering?

2. Why is it important to consider the character of those we seek advice from?

3. According to the criteria given in 3:10-11, who do you know that you might go to for advice?

4. How was Timothy to evaluate the advice he received from others, including Paul (3:14-15)?

5. Why was Paul such a good mentor for Timothy?

6. Focus on 3:15-17. What is the purpose of Scripture?

7. How can Scripture be used in helping us to make decisions?

8. How might Scripture be misused in decision making?

How can you avoid this?

---

9. What does good advice consist of according to 4:1-2?

---

10. Why might some people be motivated to give bad advice?

---

11. How can you avoid having "itchy ears" (4:3) as you seek advice?

---

12. How will this study change the way in which you seek advice?

Pray for God's guidance as you study Scripture and seek advice.

Now or Later

A contrast between people with "itchy ears" and people who know how to accept advice is found in Acts. *Read Acts 17:1-12.*

In what ways does Paul follow the principles of good advice you discovered in 2 Timothy?

Why did the people of Thessalonica not listen to Paul's advice?

How is this similar to the people with "itchy ears" in 2 Timothy?

How is it similar to people in your community?

What is commendable about the Berean style of evaluating advice?

Have you been more like a Thessalonian or a Berean in accepting advice?

6

Keep On Praying

Billy Graham has said, "Heaven is full of answers to prayers for which no one ever bothered to ask."

GROUP DISCUSSION. What has been your most amazing answer to prayer?

PERSONAL REFLECTION. Corrie ten Boom once asked, "Is prayer your steering wheel or your spare tire?" How would you have answered her?

Although most Christians believe in praying about important decisions, they often make their decisions without prayer. There are many reasons for this: They question whether the particular decision they are facing requires prayer. They do not have time to pray because a decision is needed immediately. They do not know what to ask. They don't really believe that God will give them an answer. Even Jesus' closest disciples needed instruction in prayer. *Read Luke 11:1-13.*

1. What one idea about prayer stands out to you the most in these verses?

2. What kinds of things does Jesus tell us we should pray for in verses 2-4?

3. Which of these has been most prominent and most lacking in your own prayer life?

4. How would you feel about a friend who would be so persistent in bothering you in the middle of the night (vv. 5-8)?

5. How would you characterize the awakened neighbor?

6. How does the awakened neighbor differ from God?

7. In what ways are we to be like the persistent neighbor?

---

8. How are we to practice asking, seeking and knocking?

---

9. What assurance do we have that God will give us good gifts (vv. 11-13)?

---

10. *Read Luke 18:1-8.* Why would Jesus compare God to an unjust judge?

How does this comparison help Jesus to make his point?

---

11. When in your prayer life have you felt like the widow in this parable?

How do you think that God would prefer that you pray?

12. How do the lessons of these parables apply to your prayers concerning your decisions?

Thank God for his past answers to your prayers and ask again for his guidance in the decisions you face.

Now or Later

"Reading a book about prayer, listening to lectures and talking about it is very good, but it won't teach you to pray. You get nothing without exercise, without practice. I might listen for a year to a professor of music playing the most beautiful music, but that won't teach me to play an instrument" (Andrew Murray, "The Spiritual Life," *Christianity Today* 34, no. 2).

Spend time in prayer on your own, with a prayer partner or with a small group.

7

How Does God Speak?

John 14:15-27

It is very easy for us to confuse our wishes with God's leading. Is it possible to be certain that it is God who has spoken and not our hearts playing tricks on us?

GROUP DISCUSSION. Be creative as you work together in making a list of "Top Ten Ways to Know God Has Spoken."

PERSONAL REFLECTION. How would your life be different if every decision you made was based solely on the feelings of your heart?

Just before going to the cross, Jesus spoke to his confused disciples and assured them that he would continue to lead and guide them. He said that he would give them two signs to show them that they were going in the right direction: love and the Spirit. *Read John 14:15-27.*

1. What promise in this passage gives you the greatest sense of assurance?

2. How will we recognize our love for God and his love for us?

---

3. Looking back at your last major decision, how did it demonstrate your love for Christ?

---

4. What facts are given about the identity of the Spirit?

---

5. What is Jesus' purpose in having the Spirit sent to us?

---

6. What help can we expect from the Holy Spirit in making decisions?

7. Describe a time when you have known that the Holy Spirit was counseling you.

8. How does Jesus answer Judas's question, "But, Lord, why do you intend to show yourself to us and not to the world?" (v. 22)?

9. Describe the special relationship you have with Christ. What has he shown you?

How have you felt his love?

10. What kind of peace is Jesus talking about in verse 27?

How does it differ from the world's version of peace?

11. Dietrich Bonhoeffer, who was executed by the Nazis for his faith, said, "Peace is the opposite of security." What does it mean to have peace about a decision you have made?

12. What have Jesus' words in this passage taught you about identifying God's voice?

Pray for the ability to discern the presence of the Holy Spirit in your life.

Now or Later

Moses had trouble believing that it was really God who was telling him to lead the Israelites out of Egypt. *Read about Moses' call in Exodus 3:1-12.*

If you had been Moses, how would you have reacted to the sign of authenticity that God gave in verse 12?

When have you received God's after-the-fact assurance regarding a decision you have made?

Read Exodus 4:1-17. What additional signs of assurance does God give to Moses?

Why do you think Moses had so much trouble believing God?

What can you learn from Moses' struggle?

8

What If I Make the Wrong Decision?

Genesis 16

A major barrier to making a decision can be the fear of making the wrong choice.

GROUP DISCUSSION. On a scale of 1-10 (1 = I'm sure everything will work out; 10 = A wrong decision will destroy my entire life), how fearful are you about making a wrong decision?

What experiences in your life have contributed to or relieved your fears?

PERSONAL REFLECTION. Think of the worst decision you have made. Why was it wrong?

God had promised Abram and Sarai that they would have many descendants and become a great nation. On the basis of this promise, Abram had left everything familiar and had followed God to the strange land of Canaan. However, after living there for ten years, Abram and Sarai were still childless (and at eighty-five years old, well past their childbearing years). Impatient with God's failure to act, they made a desperate decision.

Read Genesis 16.

1. Which character in this story are you most like and why? (Sarai—regretful of a decision you have made? Abram—wondering what went wrong? Hagar—blamed for someone else's bad choice? Ishmael—the product of others' dysfunction?)

2. What decisions do Sarai and Abram make in this story?

3. Looking at these decisions from our perspective, several millennia after the fact, why were these decisions so flawed?

4. Why do you think Abram and Sarai believed these decisions to be for the best?

5. What were the consequences of Abram and Sarai's decisions for themselves?

for Hagar?

for the world?

6. What have been the consequences of your worst decisions?

7. Where does Sarai place the blame for her troubles?

8. Why do you think people are reluctant to take responsibility for their decisions?

9. What good does God bring out of these bad decisions?

10. Why did God intervene instead of simply letting everyone live with the mess they had made?

11. After reading this report of Abram and Sarai's mistake, what can you expect God to do with your own bad decisions?

12. What is comforting about being seen by God, even at our worst moments (v. 13)?

Confess to God the mistakes you have made and ask him to bring good from them.

Now or Later

King David seemed to make as many bad decisions as he did wise ones. He tried to hide from King Saul by living among the enemies of Israel and almost had to go to war against his own people (1 Samuel 27—29), he committed adultery and covered it up with murder (2 Samuel 11—12), he contributed to a family feud (2 Samuel 13—14), and he took a census of Israel and Judah (2 Samuel 24). *Read what he has to say about finding forgiveness for our bad decisions in Psalm 32.*

According to this psalm, what should we do about our bad or sinful decisions?

What will happen if we do not come to God with our mistakes?

What will happen if we do?

In what ways have you acted like a horse or a mule (v. 9)?

9

Worry-Free Decisions

Luke 12:13-34

Have you ever given a friend a gift that you knew was exactly right? Remember how good it felt to see the joy in your friend as he or she opened the gift. Wouldn't it feel good to experience God's pleasure over a decision you have made, never having to worry whether you have done the right thing?

GROUP DISCUSSION. Describe something you did that brought real pleasure to another person. What has someone done for you that pleased you?

PERSONAL REFLECTION. Who have you been attempting to please? How have you been going about it?

When a man came to Jesus upset about an inheritance, Jesus took the opportunity to talk with his disciples about pleasing God instead of worrying about self. *Read Luke 12:13-34.*

1. Describe the man in verse 13. What were his worries?

2. What do the people of our society worry about?

_____

3. What impact do our worries have on our decisions?

_____

4. Why wouldn't Jesus help the man in this story?

_____

5. To what extent has "the abundance of possessions" been an ingredient in your decision-making process?

_____

6. The rich man thought he had made a worry-free decision (v. 19). Why was he called a fool (v. 20)?

7. The rich man did have a problem that needed to be solved (v. 17). What decisions could he have made that Jesus would have found pleasing?

---

8. Why are ravens and lilies so carefree?

---

9. What would be different about making a decision from a raven or lily's point of view?

---

10. How does our worry dishonor God?

---

11. What does it mean to seek the kingdom of God (v. 31) and provide a treasure in heaven (v. 33)?

12. How have you sought God's kingdom as you have been making decisions?

Pray about everything that worries you, putting it into God's hands again.

Now or Later

Doubt can often be the same as worry. *Read what James has to say about this in James 1:2-8.*

According to these verses, why are some people confused?

Why is a wave an apt description of a doubter?

What advice does James give us for dealing with doubt and worry?

Leader's Notes

Leading a Bible discussion can be an enjoyable and rewarding experience. But it can also be *scary*—especially if you've never done it before. If this is your feeling, you're in good company. When God asked Moses to lead the Israelites out of Egypt, he replied, "O Lord, please send someone else to do it"! (Ex 4:13). It was the same with Solomon, Jeremiah and Timothy, but God helped these people in spite of their weaknesses, and he will help you as well.

You don't need to be an expert on the Bible or a trained teacher to lead a Bible discussion. The idea behind these inductive studies is that the leader guides group members to discover for themselves what the Bible has to say. This method of learning will allow group members to remember much more of what is said than a lecture would.

These studies are designed to be led easily. As a matter of fact, the flow of questions through the passage from observation to interpretation to application is so natural that you may feel that the studies lead themselves. This study guide is also flexible. You can use it with a variety of groups—student, professional, neighborhood or church groups. Each study takes forty-five to sixty minutes in a group setting.

There are some important facts to know about group dynamics and encouraging discussion. The suggestions listed below should enable you to effectively and enjoyably fulfill your role as leader.

Preparing for the Study

1. Ask God to help you understand and apply the passage in your own life. Unless this happens, you will not be prepared to lead others. Pray too for the various members of the group. Ask God to open your hearts to the message of his Word and motivate you to action.

2. Read the introduction to the entire guide to get an overview of the entire book and the issues which will be explored.

3. As you begin each study, read and reread the assigned Bible passage to familiarize yourself with it.

4. This study guide is based on the New International Version of the Bible. It will help you and the group if you use this translation as the basis for your study and discussion.

5. Carefully work through each question in the study. Spend time in meditation and reflection as you consider how to respond.

6. Write your thoughts and responses in the space provided in the study guide. This will help you to express your understanding of the passage clearly.

7. It might help to have a Bible dictionary handy. Use it to look up any unfamiliar words, names or places. (For additional help on how to study a passage, see chapter five of *How to Lead a LifeBuilder Study,* IVP, 2018.)

8. Consider how you can apply the Scripture to your life. Remember that the group will follow your lead in responding to the studies. They will not go any deeper than you do.

9. Once you have finished your own study of the passage, familiarize yourself with the leader's notes for the study you are leading. These are designed to help you in several ways. First, they tell you the purpose the study guide author had in mind when writing the study. Take time to think through how the study questions work together to accomplish that purpose. Second, the notes provide you with additional background information or suggestions on group dynamics for various questions. This information can be useful when people have difficulty understanding or answering a question. Third, the leader's notes can alert you to potential problems you may encounter during the study.

10. If you wish to remind yourself of anything mentioned in the leader's notes, make a note to yourself below that question in the study.

Leading the Study

1. Begin the study on time. Open with prayer, asking God to help the group to understand and apply the passage.

2. Be sure that everyone in your group has a study guide. Encourage the group to prepare beforehand for each discussion by reading the introduction to the guide and by working through the questions in the study.

3. At the beginning of your first time together, explain that these studies are meant to be discussions, not lectures. Encourage the members of the group to participate. However, do not put pressure on those who may be hesitant to speak during the first few sessions. You may want to suggest the following guidelines to your group.

☐ Stick to the topic being discussed.

☐ Your responses should be based on the verses which are the focus of the discussion and not on outside authorities such as commentaries or speakers.

☐ These studies focus on a particular passage of Scripture. Only rarely should you refer to other portions of the Bible. This allows for everyone to participate in in-depth study on equal ground.

☐ Anything said in the group is considered confidential and will not be discussed outside the group unless specific permission is given to do so.

☐ We will listen attentively to each other and provide time for each person present to talk.

☐ We will pray for each other.

4. Have a group member read the introduction at the beginning of the discussion.

5. Every session begins with a group discussion question. The question or activity is meant to be used before the passage is read. The question introduces the theme of the study and encourages group members to begin to open up. Encourage as many members as possible to participate, and be ready to get the discussion going with your own response.

This section is designed to reveal where our thoughts or feelings need to be transformed by Scripture. That is why it is especially important not to read the passage before the discussion question is asked. The passage will tend to color the honest reactions people would otherwise give because they are, of course, supposed to think the way the Bible does.

You may want to supplement the group discussion question with an icebreaker to help people to get comfortable. See the community section of the *Small Group Starter Kit* (IVP, 1995) for more ideas.

You also might want to use the personal reflection question with your group. Either allow a time of silence for people to respond individually or discuss it together.

6. Have a group member (or members if the passage is long) read aloud the passage to be studied. Then give people several minutes to read the passage again silently so that they can take it all in.

7. Question 1 will generally be an overview question designed to briefly survey the passage. Encourage the group to look at the whole passage, but try to avoid getting sidetracked by questions or issues that will be addressed later in the study.

8. As you ask the questions, keep in mind that they are designed to be used just as they are written. You may simply read them aloud. Or you may prefer to express them in your own words.

There may be times when it is appropriate to deviate from the study guide. For example, a question may have already been answered. If so, move on to the next question. Or someone may raise an important question not covered in the guide. Take time to discuss it, but try to keep the group from going off on tangents.

9. Avoid answering your own questions. If necessary, repeat or rephrase them until they are clearly understood. Or point out something you read in the leader's notes to clarify the context or meaning. An eager group quickly becomes passive and silent if they think the leader will do most of the talking.

10. Don't be afraid of silence. People may need time to think about the question before formulating their answers.

11. Don't be content with just one answer. Ask, "What do the rest of you think?" or "Anything else?" until several people have given answers to the question.

12. Acknowledge all contributions. Try to be affirming whenever possible. Never reject an answer. If it is clearly off-base, ask, "Which verse led you to that conclusion?" or again, "What do the rest of you think?"

13. Don't expect every answer to be addressed to you, even though this will probably happen at first. As group members become more at ease, they will begin to truly interact with each other. This is one sign of healthy discussion.

14. Don't be afraid of controversy. It can be very stimulating. If you don't resolve an issue completely, don't be frustrated. Move on and keep it in mind for later. A subsequent study may solve the problem.

15. Periodically summarize what the group has said about the passage. This helps to draw together the various ideas mentioned and gives continuity to the study. But don't preach.

16. At the end of the Bible discussion you may want to allow group members a time of quiet to work on an idea under "Now or Later." Then discuss what you experienced. Or you may want to encourage group members to work on these ideas between meetings. Give an opportunity during the session for people to talk about what they are learning.

17. Conclude your time together with conversational prayer, adapting the prayer suggestion at the end of the study to your group. Ask for God's help in following through on the commitments you've made.

18. End on time.

Many more suggestions and helps are found in *How to Lead a LifeBuilder Study.*

Components of Small Groups
A healthy small group should do more than study the Bible. There are four components to consider as you structure your time together.

Nurture. Small groups help us to grow in our knowledge and love of God. Bible study is the key to making this happen and is the foundation of your small group.

Community. Small groups are a great place to develop deep friendships with other Christians. Allow time for informal interaction before and after each study. Plan activities and games that will help you get to know each other. Spend time having fun together—going on a picnic or cooking dinner together.

Worship and prayer. Your study will be enhanced by spending time praising God together in prayer or song. Pray for each other's needs—and keep track of how God is answering prayer in your group. Ask God to help you to apply what you are learning in your study.

Outreach. Reaching out to others can be a practical way of applying what you are learning, and it will keep your group from becoming self-focused. Host a series of evangelistic discussions for your friends or neighbors. Clean up the yard of an elderly friend. Serve at a soup kitchen together, or spend a day working in the community.

Many more suggestions and helps in each of these areas are found in the *Small Group Starter Kit.* You will also find information on building a small group. Reading through the starter kit will be worth your time.

Study 1.
Why Is God Silent? Isaiah 58.
Purpose: To show that our sinfulness has blocked communication with God and to see that he will direct us as we obey.
Question 1. The return to Jerusalem had not proven to be the grand, all-transforming experience the people had expected. Fresh troubles continued to make life just as hard or harder than it had been in captivity. The people were asking for God's help but felt that he was ignoring them.
Question 3. The phrases "they seek me out," "ask me for just decisions" and "we humbled ourselves" (vv. 2-3) indicate that the people have come to God with many forms of worship in addition to fasting. They have also

prayed, cried out, put on sackcloth and wept.

Question 5. All of the fasting and praying was only an external form. The people said words and went through motions that would make it look as if they were repentant and humble before God. In reality, the people were absorbed in seeking their own selfish pleasures, even while they appeared to be worshiping God.

Question 6. In fasting that pleases God, actions directed toward God are combined with actions directed toward people. This is expressed in several ways, such as providing food, shelter and clothing. However, of all the conceivable acts of caring, setting people free from bondage seems to be the most important in this passage. The people were to remember that they themselves had recently been living in exile. They had often been told, "Remember that you were a slave in Egypt." God wanted them to have the compassion for others that had been shown to them.

Question 7. Isaiah 59:2 states, "But your iniquities have separated you from your God; your sins have hidden his face from you, so that he will not hear." It may be helpful to think of a light switch. Ignoring God's concern for justice is like turning off the switch and breaking our contact with God. Heeding God's concern is like turning on the switch and restoring contact.

Question 8. For the people of the Old Testament, salvation was not thought of as a state of bliss, but as living in constant dialogue with God. It is this intimacy with God that is being promised here. Notice that some of the promises are for individuals (as in verses 8-10), while other promises are for the nation (vv. 11-12).

Question 9. God wants signs of right character in those whose prayers he answers, for such character is the only guarantee that what he gives is rightly accepted and rightly used.

Now or Later. This is a fairly lengthy passage. You will probably either want to suggest that people study it on their own between sessions or take an extra session to discuss it.

Study 2. Hard & Painful Decisions. Acts 20:17—21:14.

Purpose: To observe a case study of how God enabled a person to follow his will even when it was painful.

Question 2. "His overriding concern is not at all costs to survive, but rather that he may finish the race and complete his Christ-given task of bearing witness to the good news of God's grace" (John R. W. Stott, *The Message of Acts* [Downers Grove, Ill.: InterVarsity Press, 1990], p. 326).

Question 3. The words of Thomas à Kempis may be helpful in answering this question. He wrote:

> Jesus hath now many lovers of his heavenly kingdom, but few bearers of his cross. He hath many desirous of comfort, but few of tribulation. He findeth many companions of his table, but few of his abstinence. All desire to rejoice with him, few are willing to endure anything for him. Many follow Jesus unto the breaking of bread; but few to the drinking of the cup of his passion. . . . Many love Jesus so long as adversities do not happen. Many praise and bless him, so long as they receive comforts from him. (*The Imitation of Christ* [Chicago: Moody Press, 1980], pp. 114-15)

Question 6. The warnings were given not to discourage Paul, but to warn him. John Stott draws a distinction between a prediction and a prohibition:

> The better solution is to draw a distinction between a prediction and a prohibition. Certainly Agabus only predicted that Paul would be bound and handed over to the Gentiles (21:11); the pleadings with Paul which followed are not attributed to the Spirit and may have been the fallible (indeed mistaken) human deduction from the Spirit's prophecy. For if Paul had heeded his friends' pleas, then Agabus' prophecy would not have been fulfilled! It is more difficult to understand 21:4 in this way, since the "urging" itself is said to be "through the Spirit." But perhaps Luke's statement is a condensed way of saying that the warning was divine while the urging was human. After all, the Spirit's word to Paul combined the compulsion to go with a warning of the consequences (20:22-23). (Stott, *Message of Acts*, p. 333)

Question 7. Even though Paul's friends mistook the prophecy of hardship and imminent suffering for a sign that God did not want Paul in Jerusalem, they were still used as God's agents of encouragement. They gave a message from the Holy Spirit that confirmed the one Paul had already received, they demonstrated that Paul was deeply loved by them and by God, and they prayed with him.

Question 9. "To know God's will we must first accept God's salvation in Christ. It is God's will that none should perish. Second, to know God's will we must be obedient to God's word as recorded in the Scriptures. We find 90 percent of God's will right there. Third, to know God's will we must pray and earnestly seek His direction. Fourth, to know God's will we must listen to the voice of the Holy Spirit" (George and Donald Sweeting, *The Acts of God* [Chicago: Moody Press, 1986], p. 173).

Question 11. When the people said, "The Lord's will be done," they were making a positive affirmation, not a feeble resignation. To make such a statement is a cry of faith and trust that "God is good, all the time!"

Study 3. God's Unique Plan. Romans 12.
Purpose: To show that much of God's will for our lives will be discovered as we use our bodies and minds as God created them to be used.
Question 1. John Stott makes the following comments about the living sacrifice:

> It is not to be offered in the temple courts or in the church building, but rather in home life and in the marketplace. It is the presentation of our bodies to God. This blunt reference to our bodies was calculated to shock some of Paul's Greek readers. Brought up on Platonic thought, they will have regarded the body as an embarrassing encumbrance. . . . Still today some Christians feel self-conscious about their bodies. The traditional evangelical invitation is that we give our "hearts" to God, not our "bodies." . . . But Paul is clear that the presentation of our bodies is our spiritual act of worship. It is a significant Christian paradox. No worship is pleasing to God which is purely inward, abstract and mystical; it must express itself in concrete acts of service performed by our bodies. (*Romans* [Downers Grove, Ill.: InterVarsity Press, 1994], pp. 321-22)

Question 2. "These two value systems (this world and God's will) are incomparable, even in direct collision with one another. Whether we are thinking about the purpose of life or the meaning of life, about how to measure greatness or how to respond to evil, about ambition, sex, honesty, money, community, religion or anything else, the two sets of standards diverge so completely that there is no possibility of compromise. No wonder Karl Barth called Christian ethics 'the great disturbance,' so violently does it challenge, interrupt and upset the tranquil status quo" (Stott, *Romans*, pp. 323-24).
Question 3. "Because human beings are inveterate conformists, the temptation to simply fit into the picture and fade into the scenery can be practically overwhelming. The committed life, however, is shown by the degree in which the believer stays in the secular world without being trapped by it and without failing to be a witness to it. The tension is aptly described by the Master's words explaining that we are 'in the world but not of it'" (Stuart Briscoe, *Romans* [Waco, Tex.: Word, 1982], p. 216).
Question 5. "[Paul] does not promise that the careless, the casual, and

the uncommitted will somehow land on their feet and find out that they did God's will by accident. Rather he states that those who genuinely do what is required will find in their own experience the reality of the sweet will of God" (Briscoe, *Romans,* p. 217).

Question 6. "Diversity, not uniformity, is the mark of God's handiwork. It is so in nature; it is so in grace, too, and nowhere more so than in the Christian community. Here are many men and women with the most diverse kinds of parentage, environment, temperament, and capacity. Not only so, but since they became Christians they have been endowed by God with a great variety of spiritual gifts as well. Yet because and by means of that diversity, all can co-operate for the good of the whole" (F. F. Bruce, *The Epistle of Paul to the Romans* [Grand Rapids, Mich.: Eerdmans, 1963], p. 227).

Question 7. "By this expression Paul means that God equips each believer for a particular task and expects him to discover and fulfill his special role in the context of the believing community. Once this is understood, the believer is delivered from a number of potential miscalculations. He will not aspire to be more than God intends him to be, but he will not settle for being less than he was created and redeemed to be. Accordingly, he will be delivered from an arrogance which is destructive of harmony in the body of believers and will be content to make a 'sober' evaluation of his own gifts and calling" (Briscoe, *Romans,* p. 217).

Question 11. "Mutual love, sympathy and honor within the brotherhood of believers are to be expected, but something more is enjoined here— love and forgiveness to those outside the fellowship, and not least to those who persecute them and wish them ill" (Bruce, *Epistle of Paul,* p. 228).

Question 13. As the leader, you may wish to read verses 9-21 aloud, pausing after each phrase to allow the members of your group to respond silently to God. Their response could be either, "Thank you, Lord, for the transformation in my life," or "I confess that I have been conformed to the world."

Study 4. The Anatomy of a Wise Decision. Proverbs 3:1-26.
Purpose: To help group members recognize the factors that make for a wise decision.

Question 2. Wise decisions consist of following wise teaching, being motivated by love and faithfulness, trusting in the Lord, going God's way instead of our way, giving to God generously, and submitting to God's dis-

56 ———————————————————————————————— *Decisions*

cipline. A decision made on the basis of these criteria is promised to
bring great reward.

Question 3. A decision that is based on love and faithfulness is given the
promise of winning favor with God and humanity. A decision that is not
motivated by love and faithfulness will allow us to become self-serving.

Question 4. Verses 5-8 "are to Christ's disciples what the wedding cere-
mony is to newlyweds. They spell out what is and is not to be done
within the relationship. They set the terms of what it means to live with
God at the outset of our commitment to Him and through every step of
our pilgrimage. They are the 'to have and to hold from this day forward'
of our marriage-covenant with God" (David Hubbard, *Proverbs* [Waco,
Tex.: Word, 1989], p. 70).

Question 5. The principle of firstfruits comes from Deuteronomy 26:1-
15. It is the practice of giving God the first produce to ripen and be harvested. To give the firstfruits is an act of trust because the giver has no
guarantee that the rest of the crop will actually be harvested. "Prosperity,
gratitude, and charity are an indivisible triad of experiences in biblical
thought, and notably in Proverbs" (Hubbard, *Proverbs,* p. 72).

Question 6. To "despise" and "reject" God's discipline is the opposite of
the trust that is spoken of in verses 5-8. People despise discipline when
they live in denial, make excuses or pass blame.

Question 8. Wisdom is valuable because it provides understanding,
brings prosperity, lengthens a person's life and gives peace.

Question 10. We know that our world is a fruit of God's wisdom (vv. 19-
20). Since we can clearly see what God's wisdom has already accomplished,
the author now assures us of what it can do for each of us personally. Wisdom will give us life, keep us safe, banish fear and build our confidence.

Study 5. Good Advice. 2 Timothy 3:10—4:8.
Purpose: To help group members learn to distinguish between good and
bad advice.
Questions 1-2. John Stott suggests:

> No, Paul is not boasting. He has reasons quite other than exhibitionism for
> drawing attention to himself. He mentions his teaching first, and then goes
> on to supply two objective evidences of the genuineness of his teaching,
> namely the life he lived and the sufferings he endured. Indeed, these are
> good (though not infallible) general tests of a person's sincerity, and even of
> the truth or falsehood of his system. Is he so convinced of his position that
> he both practises what he preaches and is prepared to suffer for it? Have his

beliefs made him a better man, even in the face of opposition? Paul could answer both questions affirmatively. The false teachers lived lives of self-indulgence, and it would be quite out of character to expect them to be willing to suffer for their views; they were altogether too soft and easy-going for that. The apostle Paul, however, lived a consistent life of right-eousness, self-control, faith and love, and remained steadfast to his princi-ples through many and grievous persecution. (*Guard the Gospel* [Downers Grove, Ill.: InterVarsity Press, 1973], pp. 94-95)

Question 4. Timothy is told to evaluate what others say based on the convictions he has built over time. Those convictions have been given to him by Scripture and by people whose character he knows and trusts— namely his mother, his grandmother and Paul. A Christian must stand firm on what he knows of the truth, like a rock resists the increasing fury of the waves.

Question 6. Paul says that Scripture will make us "wise for salvation through faith in Christ Jesus" (v. 15). By this he means, "the Bible is essentially a handbook of salvation. Its over-arching purpose is to teach not facts of science (e.g. the nature of moon rock) which men can dis-cover by their own empirical investigation, but facts of salvation, which no space exploration can discover but only God can reveal" (Stott, *Guard the Gospel*, p. 102). Paul goes on to show that Scripture teaches us both what to believe and how to behave.

Question 7. Since Scripture teaches us how to behave, all such teaching will come to bear on our decisions. We should never make a decision that will cause us to act or believe in a way that is contrary to Scripture.

Question 8. This question is not directly answered in the passage, but by understanding the purposes of Scripture, we will also come to under-stand what it is not intended to do. The Bible generally teaches principles of behavior that will guide us in reaching a decision. For example, if a person is considering whether or not to marry a particular person, the Bible can help the couple examine their motives and desires. The Bible cannot be expected to give a yes or no answer as if it were a crystal ball.

Question 9. Good advice will (1) take into account that Christ is coming back and will judge us for what we have done; (2) be relevant in that it will correct, rebuke and encourage according to the needs of the one being advised; (3) be patient so that it will not pressure or attempt to contrive a decision; and (4) contain careful instruction which guides a person intellectually.

Question 10. Paul warns that people will substitute their own desires for

God's truth. They will judge teachers by their own subjective taste instead of by the authority of God's Word. In order to be popular or to gain an audience, teachers will be tempted to say what people want to hear.

Study 6. Keep On Praying. Luke 11:1-13; 18:1-8.
Purpose: To encourage group members to keep praying about the decisions they face.
Question 2. The petitions of the Lord's Prayer include "Father, hallowed be your name"—a request for a proper attitude toward God; "your kingdom come"—a desire for God's kingdom to be fully realized; "give us each day our daily bread"—acknowledgment of our continual dependence on God; "forgive us our sins, for we also forgive everyone who sins against us"—a recognition of the need to forgive and be forgiven; "and lead us not into temptation"—a realization of our weakness and the ease with which we give way to the temptations of the world.
Questions 4-5. Here's some helpful background information:

> The setting is a small village where there are no shops. A household would bake its bread each morning. Jesus pictures a man whose household has used its supply and on whom a journeying friend makes an unexpected call. It is at midnight, which probably means that the friend had travelled after dark to avoid the heat. The man must feed his friend, for hospitality was a sacred duty. So he goes to another friend for three loaves, i.e. three small loaves which would suffice for one man. But this second householder has shut his door and gone to bed with his children. Evidently he was a poor man living in a one-roomed house. The whole family would sleep on a raised platform at one end of such a room, possibly with the animals at floor level. A man in such a situation could not get up without disturbing the whole family. He raises no difficulty about giving the bread, but the bother of getting up is quite another matter. It is much easier to stay where he is. (Leon Morris, *The Gospel According to St. Luke* [Grand Rapids, Mich.: Eerdmans, 1974], p. 195)

Question 6. The point of this parable is that God is not like the awakened friend. "If even an imperfect human being, notwithstanding the inconvenience to which he is put, will arise at midnight to give a friend what he needs if he comes and asks him for help, how much more will God, the heavenly Friend, who is perfect in love, listen to the sincere prayers and supplications of His children who are really in need!" (Norval Geldenhuys, *The Gospel of Luke* [Grand Rapids, Mich.: Eerdmans, 1977], p. 324).
Question 7. "It is important that we should remember that in the parable

there is a friendship existing between the one who asks and the one who rises and gives, and that the request arises out of necessity and not out of selfishness" (Geldenhuys, *Gospel of Luke,* p. 324).

Question 8. "The lesson is clear. We must not play at prayer, but must show persistence if we do not receive the answer immediately. It is not that God is unwilling and must be pressed into answering. The whole context makes it clear that He is eager to give. But if we do not want what we are asking for enough to be persistent, we do not want it very much. It is not such tepid prayer that is answered" (Morris, *Gospel According to St. Luke,* p. 195).

Question 9. "No regenerate child of God should ever doubt that when he prays to God out of real need his prayer will be answered. He who doubts this does Him the greatest dishonor, for by not believing that He will give what we really need we in fact appear to regard Him as less sympathetic and less faithful than an ordinary earthly friend. Therefore unbelief in relation to the answering of prayer is not only a weakness, but a serious sin and utter folly" (Geldenhuys, *Gospel of Luke,* p. 325).

Question 10. Jesus is certainly not suggesting that God is like the unjust judge. This is a parable of contrasts. If a wicked man can sometimes be cajoled into doing something good, then how much more will God do right.

Question 11. The widow stands in "sharp contrast to the elect of God who call upon Him in prayer. In the eye of the unjust judge she is an unknown, troublesome person in whom he takes no interest and about whose fate he does not worry. But the chosen ones of God are well known to Him and loved by Him, and He takes the keenest interest in them" (Geldenhuys, *Gospel of Luke,* p. 447).

Now or Later. Have each member of the group sit or kneel in the center of the room while he or she is lifted to God in prayer.

Study 7. How Does God Speak? John 14:15-27.

Purpose: To learn to identify the means God uses to direct us.

Question 2. Leon Morris suggests:

> Obedience is the mark of true love. The man who truly loves Christ in this way will be loved of the Father. It might be possible to understand from this that the Father's love is thus merited. But this is not the thought of the passage. Jesus is saying in the first place that love to Him is not a thing of words. If it is real it is shown in deeds. The lover keeps the commandments of the loved one. He is also saying that the Father is not indifferent to the attitude men take to the Son. This does not mean that He hands out rewards on the basis of merit. It means rather that love calls to love. Not

only will the Father love such a man, but Jesus also will love Him. He further says that He will "manifest" Himself to them. He does not explain what this means. He simply says that in some undefined way He will reveal Himself to the man who loves Him." (*The Gospel According to John* [Grand Rapids, Mich.: Eerdmans, 1971], p. 653)

Question 4. The Spirit is given the names Counselor (v. 16), Spirit of Truth (v. 17) and Holy Spirit (v. 26). These names reflect his character. His origin is revealed in the phrase, "whom the Father will send in my name" (v. 26). His purpose is given in the words, "he lives with you and will be in you" (v. 17), "will teach you all things" (v. 26) and "will remind you of everything I have said to you" (v. 26).

Question 5. Leon Morris focuses on the importance of the Spirit as teacher:

> "All things" is comprehensive and probably means "all that you will need to know." The Spirit is to be the guide and teacher of the church. In addition to this he will bring back to the disciples' memory all the things that Jesus had told them. John has made it clear that the disciples did not grasp the significance of a good deal that their Master taught them. It seems likely that they let slip some of the things they did not understand. . . . Jesus is now saying that the Holy Spirit will supply their lack. (*Gospel According to John,* pp. 656-57).

Question 6. Sometimes the Holy Spirit will tell a person exactly what they should do. Many people can tell about a time when guidance has been clear and specific. However, even when we are not given such specific answers, the Holy Spirit will at least teach us everything that God wants us to know in making a decision and will remind us of the knowledge we already have that bears on our decision.

Question 8. Judas asks this question with the expectation that the Messiah was supposed to reveal himself in a glorious way to all humankind. Jesus' statements were causing him to fear that something had happened to disrupt God's plan. The answer to Judas' question is that love is the method of seeing. Those who love Jesus will continually be able to see him and those who do not love him will never be able to see him. The problem is not that Jesus has not been revealed, but that some do not have the eyes to see him.

Question 10. "The peace of which he speaks is not dependent on any outward circumstances, as any peace the world can give must necessarily be. Because He gives men such a peace Jesus can enjoin them not to be troubled in heart nor cowardly. A Christ-given serenity excludes both. It is worth noting that in the Bible 'peace' is given a wider and deeper meaning than in other Greek writings. For the Greeks (as for us) peace was essentially negative, the absence of war. But for the Hebrews it meant positive blessing, especially a right relationship with God" (Morris, *Gospel According to John,* p. 658).

Now or Later. You may want to consider doing this section as a separate session.

Study 8. What If I Make the Wrong Decision? Genesis 16.

Purpose: To give assurance that God will love us and use us even when we make bad decisions.

Question 2. Abram and Sarai "decided to resort to surrogate marriage, which was a perfectly respectable practice in the other cultures of the ancient Near East. A child born to a slave-girl could be regarded as the wife's own child, if she had no children of her own. Many in ancient times saw nothing wrong in surrogate marriage, and surrogate motherhood is still an issue in contemporary society. Genesis, however, clearly does not agree with the practice" (G. J. Wenham, J. A. Motyer, D. A. Carson, and R. T. France, eds., *New Bible Commentary* [Downers Grove, Ill.: InterVarsity Press, 1994], p. 72).

Question 3. Abram had slipped from faith and allowed himself to be guided by reason and the voice of his wife. "Each of the three characters displays the untruth that is part of sin, in false pride (4), false blame (5), false neutrality (6); but Sarai's mask soon slipped (6b), to show the hatred behind the talk of justice" (Derek Kidner, *Genesis* [Downers Grove, Ill.: InterVarsity Press, 1967], p. 126).

Question 5. "The obvious evils which resulted are . . . the fracturing of otherwise proper interpersonal relationships between Sarai and Hagar with the accompanying damage to Sarai's dignity and the production of contempt for Sarai from Hagar. Hagar is 'used,' but Sarai is not truly benefitted. . . . Contempt, as well as a son who turned from Abram's way, was Sarai's heritage for failure to wait for Yahweh to fulfill in His way the promise of seed" (Harold Stigers, *A Commentary on Genesis* [Grand Rapids, Mich.: Zondervan, 1976], pp. 161-62). Ishmael is considered to be the father of the Arabs and Abram's subsequent son, Isaac, to be the father of the Jews—a rivalry that continues to the present day.

Question 7. Notice that Sarai first places the blame on God when she says, "The Lord has kept me from having children" (v. 2). Then, when she gets her way, she blames both Abram and Hagar ("You are responsible for the wrong I am suffering. I put my servant in your arms, and now that she knows she is pregnant, she despises me" [v. 5]).

Question 9. God's mercy brings good out of human folly. A promise was given to Hagar that was similar to the promise given to Abram. When Ishmael is called "a wild donkey of a man (v. 12)," this is "not in the sense of a boorish, desert yokel, but in another sense. A man would not be derogated by this epithet, for the ass was a prized animal; a man so designated would be a choice person. . . . Yet he will possess something of the character of the wild ass of the desert in that he will be intractable and oppose his neighbors" (Stigers, *Commentary on Genesis*, p. 162).

Question 10. This passage gives evidence of the love of God who picks us up when we fail. It is also evidence of God's determination to bring about his plans. He had made a promise to Abram that was an integral part of his greater plan of salvation. Abram's failure would not frustrate God's plan—and our bad decisions won't frustrate it either.

Question 12. Our worst moments are also our moments of greatest need. God is near to point out responsibility and offer aid in assuming it.

Study 9. Worry-Free Decisions. Luke 12:13-34.

Purpose: To help group members think about decisions from the perspective of what would please God.

Question 1. Your group will probably notice that the man is selfish and materialistic. This is especially evident if you consider what Jesus has just been talking to the crowd about in verses 1-11. You may want to ask your group how they would feel about an uneven distribution of an inheritance. This will help them recognize that they share many of this man's worries.

Questions 2-3. Help the members of your group to think about specific worries they have had and what those worries caused them to do. For example, worries about money may cause some people to seek a higher paying job and others to take out a loan.

Question 4. "The Lord refuses to fill the traditional role of judge because his mission concerns a more important question, the question of life itself. Jesus points his hearers to the importance of priorities in the quest for 'life'" (E. Earle Ellis, *The Gospel of Luke* [Greenwood, S.C.: Attic Press, 1974], p. 177). "He came to bring men to God, not to bring property to men" (Morris, *Gospel According to St. Luke*, p. 212).

Question 5. "In this parable and these pronouncements the Saviour does not condemn the possession of worldly goods as such, but what He disapproves of is the covetous and carnal attitude with regard to earthly wealth, the trust in worldly things instead of in God, and the fault of not regarding one's possessions gratefully as God's gracious gifts and using them in His service and according to His will to the glory of His name. It is not only a terrible sin to make earthly riches and worldly pleasures the main purpose in life, but also a fatal act of folly, a deadly error" (Geldenhuys, *Gospel of Luke*, pp. 355-56).

Question 7. "Notice the repeated *my* which points to an ingrained selfishness. The man is not concerned to use his wealth wisely. He is not trying to help other people. He is not even concerned to have a richer and fuller life for himself. He is concerned only with self-indulgence" (Morris, *Gospel According to St. Luke,* p. 212).

Question 9. "They should not make their chief aim or the passion of their lives the hoarding of material things. By this the Saviour does not in any way mean that they must be lazy and neglect their ordinary work and duties, but that they must not allow their hearts to become so attached to material things that their inner lives are controlled by these, and they are not to be vexed and anxious about these things. Everyone must perform his daily task, which God gives him, whole-heartedly and to the best of his ability, but the inner life of the believer must not be caught in the clutches of materialism and of anxiety with regard to worldly things" (Geldenhuys, *Gospel of Luke*, p. 358).

Question 10. Worry shows a lack of trust. When we worry about something, it is a statement that we don't believe God can or will take care of it.

Question 11. "They are to seek his kingdom, which points to a concentration on all that the kingdom involves. Disciples have pledged themselves to their Master. They must accordingly spend their time in doing His work and seeking His kingdom. This will mean trying to produce in their own lives conduct appropriate to those who have accepted the rule of God. It will also mean trying to bring others into a like way of living, for it is in this way that the kingdom grows. Jesus adds the information that when His followers concentrate on the kingdom, these things shall be yours as well. When men truly honor God, God honors their faith. His servants may not grow wealthy as the world understands riches, but they will not lack" (Morris, *Gospel According to St. Luke,* p. 215).

Donald Baker, a former staff member with InterVarsity Christian Fellowship, is pastor of First Reformed Church of Doon, Iowa and Bethel Reformed Church of Lester, Iowa. He is also the author of the LifeBuilder Bible Studies Joshua, Judges *and* 1 & 2 Thessalonians.